Anonymous

Description of Faribault and Vicinity

Anonymous

Description of Faribault and Vicinity

ISBN/EAN: 9783743325593

Manufactured in Europe, USA, Canada, Australia, Japa

Cover: Foto ©ninafisch / pixelio.de

Manufactured and distributed by brebook publishing software
(www.brebook.com)

Anonymous

Description of Faribault and Vicinity

DESCRIPTION

—OF—

FARIBAULT VICINITY

WITH ITS CHARMING COMBINATION OF HILL AND DALE, LAKE AND RIVER,
FOREST AND PRAIRIE, SHOWING VIEWS OF ITS EDUCATIONAL
INSTITUTIONS, CHURCHES, BUSINESS ESTABLISH
MENTS AND SCENERY.

ILLUSTRATED.

1884.

ISSUED BY THE CITIZENS' COMMITTEE,

FARIBAULT, RICE CO., MINN.

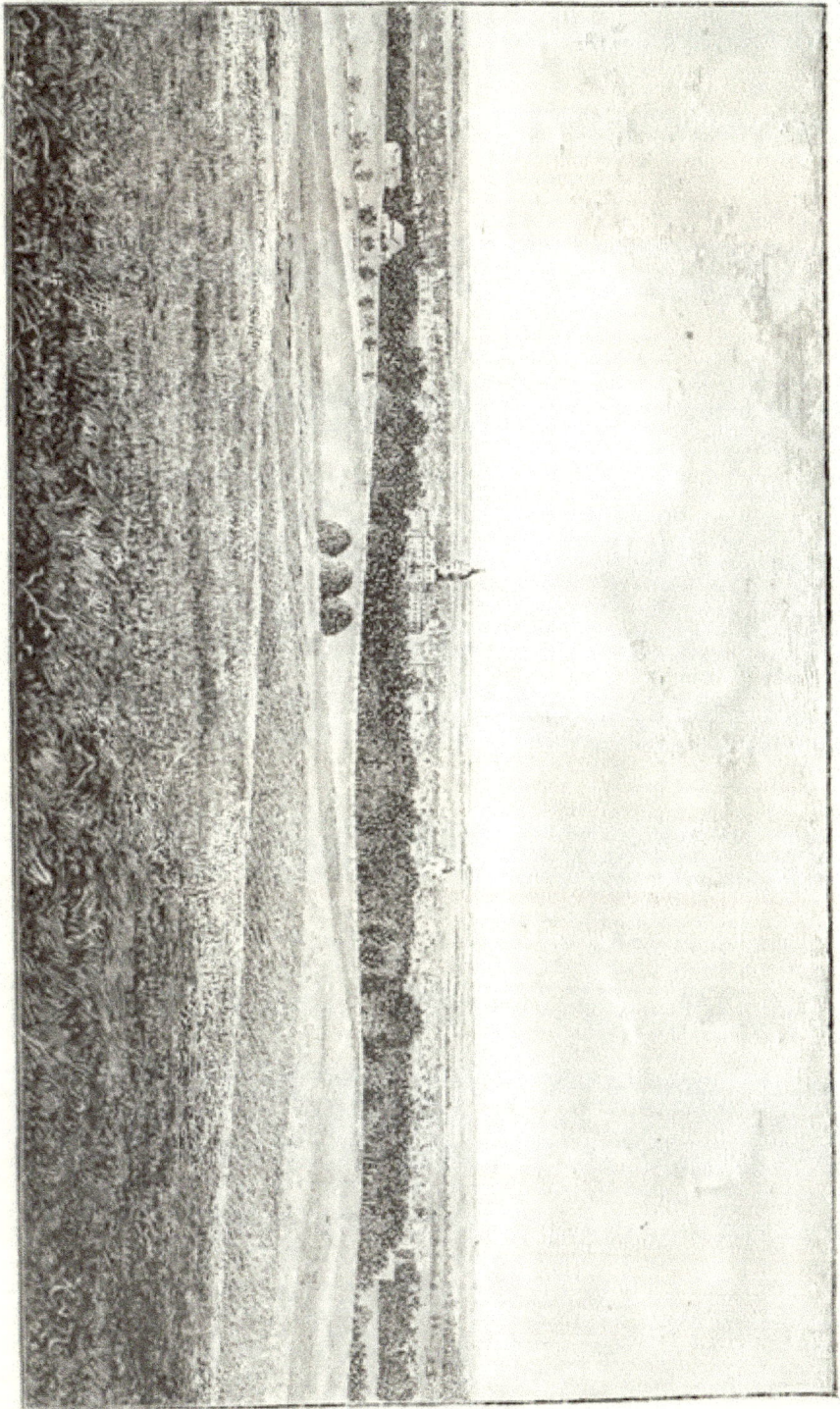

FARIBAULT FROM THE BLUFFS.

FARIBAULT AND VICINITY.

THE traveler on the Iowa Division of the Chicago, Milwaukee & St. Paul Railway, at a point directly south of St. Paul, and distant fifty-six miles from that city, comes upon one of the most charming little cities to be found anywhere in the Northwest. Both nature and art have done more for its adornment than for any other inland city or town in Minnesota. Although so well and widely known by reason of its numerous educational institutions, so little has been written or published about its natural advantages and the beauty of its surroundings, that every stranger who visits it is astonished at the size and the substantial character of the place, the great progress that has been made in the development of the public and private institutions, and the many evidences of the thrift and prosperity of its inhabitants.

Prior to its settlement by white people, the site of the future town and the charming lakes in the immediate vicinity were long the haunts and hunting and fishing grounds of the Indians. Their innate love of the beautiful, and the great abundance of fish and wild fowl that swarmed in and about these waters, then, as now, made this a favorite rendezvous. They were of the tribe of Sioux or Dakota, or, as they were known among the Indians from their forest habitations, the Wapekuti or Leaf Shooters. Their agent, Alexander Faribault, who had intermarried with them, built and occupied the first frame house before the town was established. This house is still in good repair. When the town was laid out it was named for this first inhabitant, and it has now grown to a city of about 7,000 people.

The town owes much of its attractiveness still to the charming natural scenery which so impressed even the untutored savage. It is situated a little above the junction of the Cannon and the Owatonna, or, as it is now known, the Straight Rivers: the former running in an easterly and the latter in a northerly direction. It lies mostly on the slope of the high rolling prairie that rises back to the south and the southwest from these rivers. The east bank of the Straight River is a bluff that rises more or less abruptly to the hight of a hundred feet. This bluff is surmounted by a plateau which is occupied by the six public and private institutions which are illustrated and described farther on. Back of this the receding hills rise to a farther height of 150 feet. It is from this summit that the extended view which forms the frontispiece was taken. From many points on this bluff, and from all the institutions, one can obtain a view of almost the entire city, and of the borders of the " Big Woods," which stretch away beyond the Cannon River for a distance of thirty or forty miles, forming a scene of loveliness that no artist can copy.

The reader will see from this description, that Faribault is not a western prairie town. The scenery possesses more of the characteristics of a New York or a New England town than is often found in the West. The country in all this section is broken and diversified, the soil rich, water abundant and good, and much of the higher ground is still covered with the timber. There is no section of the State that, either in town or country, offers greater inducements to those who wish to become *bona fide* settlers and citizens, than the city of Faribault and the county of Rice.

ITS INSTITUTIONS.

In 1860, when the place was only a new western town, with all that the name implies, the inhabitants were enterprising and far-seeing enough to hold out such inducements, combined with the natural advantages of the situation, as to lead Bishop Whipple to choose this for his residence. This led, of course, to the establishment here of all the schools of the Episcopal Church. The State also established here three of its most desirable and successful institutions. All of these, as will be seen, have fine large buildings of such a character that they are not only an ornament to the

ENTRANCE FROM EIGHTH STREET TO THE STATE INSTITUTION GROUNDS.

town, but they give assurance of the future growth and improvement which are sure to come, and which will make them hereafter, even more than now, an advantage to the town, both in a financial and an esthetic point of view. Probably nothing has done so much to build up the town, to preserve the even and safe financial condition of its business, or to give character and tone to the moral and social atmosphere of the people, as these institutions. They are the pride of its citizens and the admiration of all visitors, and, as we believe has been justly said of them all, "there are no schools in the country that are doing more to secure public confidence, or to give good and thorough training to those who are so fortunate as to have the advantage of it, as these schools in Faribault."

Let us set out on a visit to these schools and ramble for a little time through their beautiful grounds. Driving north along Main street till we come to Eighth street, we cross Straight River through the landscape that is shown in the accompanying view. Turning to the left, we wind around the sandstone bluff, and up the incline to the center of the beautiful and well kept grounds of

SHATTUCK SCHOOL.

As you wind in and out among the buildings and groves, and the closely shaven lawns, it is easy to see why these are looked upon as one of the most lovely spots in America for an educational

ON SHATTUCK GROUNDS.

ON SHATTUCK GROUNDS.

institution. The school was established mainly through the instrumentality of Bishop Whipple, and Drs. Breck and Manney, in 1865. It is a thorough training school for boys, and, judging from the fact that its patronage is such that it is never able to receive all who apply for admission, and that its graduates take so high a stand as they do in the eastern colleges and universities, it may justly take pride in its well earned and widespread reputation. It is chiefly a boarding school, and is so widely and well-known that it draws students from half the States of the Union.

At the same time it gives all the advantages, educational and military, to the sons of those who reside in the town. It offers, therefore, in common with the girls' school, this advantage to parents who are looking for a place of residence where they can be within reach of schools of the very highest character.

But, looking around on the grounds we have entered, we find at the left of the drive a large building of the beautiful blue limestone which is so plentiful in and about Faribault, and which furnishes the material for all of its largest and best edifices. The building we have approached is known as Shattuck Hall, in honor of Dr. Shattuck, of Boston, one of the most liberal benefactors of the church work in Faribault. It is occupied by cadets and teachers for residence and dormitories, and the basement temporarily furnishes a dining room. To the right, embowered

SHATTUCK HALL AND SCHOOL BUILDING.

in a large grove of native trees, and surrounded by beautiful lawns and flowers, and vases and statuary, is the most lovely piece of school and church architecture one can find anywhere in the West. It is the Memorial Chapel of the Good Shepherd. It was built in 1872-73 by Mrs. Shumway, of Chicago, as a memorial of her daughter, and one would travel far to find a more fitting or beautiful memorial, or one that exerts so wide an influence for good. Not only the boys and young men who daily gather there for religious instruction and divine worship are receiving impressions which are doing more than aught else, it may be, to mold the

WHIPPLE HALL—SHATTUCK.

character, and which will be among the brightest memories in the future of their happy life at Shattuck, but every citizen and every visitor who even once joins in the hearty, joyous service, as it is there rendered, carries away with him a little of the holy and the softening influence which the sacred place always throws around its worshipers. Long may it stand, to do its part in training men who shall be leaders in all that is truly manly and helpful in human life.

Retracing our steps a little, we pass the temporary frame buildings that have nearly served their purpose as school and study rooms, leaving on our right a large, handsome building of the same limestone, named in honor of the first Bishop of Minnesota, " Whipple Hall ;" we pass in the circuit the large stone building known as the Manney Armory Hall, and used as a gymnasium and bowling alley below, and a drill hall above ; and so on past the commandant's residence on the left, the fine parade ground on the right, through the grove out of the grounds to the south.

The grounds just left comprise 100 acres. They open on the south immediately into the large, fine grounds of the

STATE INSTITUTION FOR THE DEAF AND DUMB.

These have the same park-like appearance as those of Shattuck School. The State has furnished, as will be seen by reference to the view given, an elegant building. It is thoroughly equipped for the care and education of the deaf children of the State. The combined system of sign manual, oral and industrial methods is employed. embracing all the latest and most approved helps recognized in this department of popular education. No better example of the practical advantages of an indus- trial education can be found in the State than in this school for the deaf. The building is ample for all the accommodation and instruction of 200 pupils, and to the honor of the gentlemen who had the charge of its erection, it may be said, that it is one of the few public buildings the writer ever heard of that was built and furnished for less money than was appropriated for it. It is surrounded by sixty-five acres of land, is situated on one of the most prominent points on the bluff, and with its winding walks and drives is a noble testimony of the liberality of the State in the care of its unfortunates.

Proceeding on our way to the southward, we next enter the grounds of

MAXSEY ARMORY HALL, AND CAMPUS, BATTALION DRILL.—SHATTUCK. COMMANDANT'S RESIDENCE IN BACKGROUND.

ST. MARY'S HALL.

This, like Shattuck School, is a part of the educational work carried on by the Episcopal Church under the general supervision of the Bishop. It is, without doubt, one of the best and most carefully and judiciously managed institutions for the training and culture of young ladies in the country. This fact is testified to by the large and liberal patronage both from abroad and from our own citizens, and the high estimate in which the school is held by its patrons. It has but recently occupied its new and commodious building on the grounds we have just entered. Like those we have left, those who chose the location had an eye for the beautiful. It stands on a perpendicular bluff nearly opposite the main part of the town, and commands a more immediate view of the city itself than any of the others. Its grounds, when the plans of the landscape architect are carried out, will not only offer attractions to visitors, but will afford a delightful place for the free and healthful exercise of the inmates.

Continuing our way still toward the south, we pass over the highway in a deep ravine, on an iron bridge of artistic design, which was erected by the city to afford an easy access to the school from the streets below. Our way leads us on the higher ground to the east and south, for a quarter of a mile or more, when we enter the grounds of the

SEABURY DIVINITY SCHOOL.

This is the Theological School of the Episcopal Church. The building is in the mediæval style of architecture, and is most charmingly situated in a large native grove of old trees. It was a favorite site for the tepees of a band of Sioux who made their abode here and a little to the south, prior to, and indeed long after the advent of the white man. A few of their descendants are still here, though not as formerly lazily drawing out their lives in blankets and paint, but "clothed and in their right mind," and making more of an approach to the habits and industry of civilized life than the old residents of Minnesota once thought possible. This has been brought about, and so much at least done toward the peaceable solution of the much vexed Indian problem, by the earnest efforts of the Bishop, and by the same influences that have founded the schools which are now the pride and the beauty of Faribault.

Next south of the Seabury grounds, and separated from them by a deep and picturesque ravine, we again enter grounds belonging to the State. The first thing that attracts our attention is the

SCHOOL FOR THE BLIND.

This occupies the house that was till recently the residence of Mr. Alex. Faribault. A large addition has now been made to it, and it presents to the visitor a very commodious and handsome appearance. Continuing on our way, we come at a short distance to the last, but in its results, by no means the least interesting of the institutions which have made our city so far famed. This is the

SOUTH WING OF IMBECILE SCHOOL.

SHUMWAY MEMORIAL CHAPEL.—SHATTUCK.

SCHOOL FOR FEEBLE-MINDED CHILDREN.

Its establishment by the State authorities gives one renewed faith in the sympathy of human nature for its kind.   Its aim is to give these unfortunate children of nature such elementary education as they are capable of receiving, and especially to teach them to care for themselves, to work, and so to make them, so far as may be, self-supporting.   No greater charity and no more self-denying labor engages the attention of any one in all the round of public charity.

If you should continue your drive into the country, in almost any direction, with eyes open for the interesting and the beautiful, you will be hard to please if you do not return feeling that you want to go again

CEDAR LAKE.—THE ISLES.

and again.   The country is of such a nature, you can go for an afternoon's drive on the open, rolling prairie, passing everywhere fields of the most luxuriant growth of wheat, oats, corn and other grains—for Rice County farmers have learned there is money in other things than wheat—and here and there as fine herds of cattle as one would wish to see. Or you can go eastward and find hilly roads that will almost make you imagine you are back in New England again, till, after a time, you emerge into one of the largest, most fertile, and most enchanting rolling prairies to be found anywhere in the State. Or, again, if you wish, you can take to the woods, and winding in and out between woodland and field, come, with an easy drive of from three to ten miles, to some of the beautiful lakes for which Minnesota stands without a peer, and of which the neighborhood you are visiting has its full share. Then try your hand at fishing or duck shooting, as the season may suggest, and see if there is any one of the "watering places" that can fill an afternoon, or a morning, either, for that matter, so brim full of real healthy enjoyment as an excursion like this we have marked out. And the beauty of it is, that, if you want a comfortable, quiet, "go-as-you-please" place to spend the summer, where you can enjoy yourself driving, or fishing, or hunting, or lounging, according to your taste or habit, there is room enough and variety enough to give you employment for the season. The reader can see something of the sport that awaits him if he shall be so fortunate as to form one of a party such as is pictured elsewhere, of a very common summer scene at almost any of our numerous lakes. A string of two or three hundred fish, black bass, wall-eyed pike, perch, etc.; a quiet sail on the beautiful sheet of water on one of the superb summer days that so often invite away from town and business; or the picnic on the shore after the sail, and the "string" has been brought in, as shown in the illustration, has in it a zest and enjoyment that would repay a much longer ride than is necessary in order to reach it.

This brief sketch of some of the attractions of this charming inland city, and of the many points of beauty and interest in and around it, has not been made for the sake of a picture book. It has been done to show, so far as may be done on paper, the superior advantages it offers to the tourist who is looking for a place of resort for the summer; to those who are in quest of a pleasant and healthy place in which to make a home for

FISHING PARTY AT ROBERD'S LAKE.

COURT HOUSE.

their families ; to those who have children they wish to give the best possible educational advantages without sending them from home ; and to business men who are seeking in the Northwest an attractive town that offers good opportunities for business enterprises and for investments.

The citizens of Faribault feel a just pride in urging the claims of their town and of the farming country around it upon all of these classes of people. The preceding pages, with the views, which may be multiplied many times, give some idea of the natural beauties of the place and its surroundings, and of the unusual advantages grouped here in the educational and public institutions.

The town itself is not behind in the particulars which have been mentioned. The presence of the schools —State and private—has had much influence in determining the character of the people who have naturally sought homes here. A much larger proportion than is usually found in

BETHLEHEM ACADEMY.

western towns of its age are of American birth. The fact will become
more and more apparent that people of means and of culture will be at-
tracted to it as a place of residence. Besides the schools mentioned
above, it may be said as still more important to the great body of the
people, that the public schools are worthy of the highest commendation,
while the Bethlehem Academy and the parochial schools of the Church
of the Immaculate Conception are doing an admirable work in the
thoroughness and excellence of their instruction. All the churches have
excellent church buildings, and most of them good congregations. The
tasty appearance of the private dwellings and grounds, the substantial
character of the business houses, added to what has been written, and
much more that might be without exaggeration, all combine to make
Faribault an attractive, beautiful place—whether for a few days' or weeks'
sojourn, or as a permanent abiding place for one's self and family.

STATE INSTITUTE FOR THE DEAF AND DUMB.

FARIBAULT AS A BUSINESS POINT.

As it is not within the design of this pamphlet to give a statistical statement of the business of Faribault, its beautiful surroundings and educational facilities have been given great prominence, yet its advantages as a business center ought not to pass unnoticed. Indeed, the combination of superior manufacturing and commercial facilities with its attractions as a place of residence or sojourn constitute its strong claim. A brief allusion to the former, in more detail than has been given, is therefore appropriate.

Faribault is the most important station on the Iowa & Minnesota Division of the C. M. & St. P. Railway. It has connection, also, in all

ARLINGTON HOUSE.

directions, by the Cannon Valley Division of the M. & St. L. Railroad, which is operated by the Rock Island Company, thus giving it the advantage of competing routes. No town in the Northwest is in a healthier financial condition. Many of the best business men have shown their faith in its growth and prosperity by remaining here almost from the beginning. They own their business houses, and do business on their own capital. All the necessary public buildings have been erected, and there is no heavy bonded indebtedness. There is no burdensome taxation, either present or prospective. Its banks, its general mercantile business and manufacturing and milling interests, are all in good financial condition. The Brunswick Hotel, one of the handsomest and most comfortable family hotels to be found anywhere, the Arlington and the Allen House, afford ample accommodation to either transient or permanent guests.

The manufacturing enterprises which have been established have generally succeeded, and have made money for their proprietors. There has never been a disastrous failure of any legitimate business. There is abundant room and encouragement for other enterprises that will both benefit the town and will well repay the wise investment of capital and labor. Some of the most valuable water power in the place awaits improvement. Besides having a good fall, it depends for a constant flow on a river that drains a large number of the lakes in the vicinity. The State has made a land grant for the purpose of raising the outlets of these lakes, and so making them reservoirs of water, which may be stored in them till it is needed by the mills below in time of drouth. This land has been sold, and the proceeds to the amount of $30,000 are in bank, awaiting expenditure by the commissioners. There are seven good water powers in the city or its immediate vicinity, several of which will be benefited by this improvement. An abundance of poplar in the adjacent forests invites the establishment of a paper factory. Linseed oil and other works might be started and carried on with profit, the surrounding country not only being perfectly adapted to the supply of an abundance of the raw material, but the railroad facilities being such as to make it a good point for the distribution of manufactured articles of agricultural machinery, which ought to be made at home, instead of paying, as now, large profits to manufacturers and laborers in other States.

132/3 =

121

111 | 3⁶⁰

111

Valley - 5⁰⁰   11/18/30

ST. MARY'S HALL.

As the chief interest of the State has, down to the present time, or nearly, been that of wheat production, the manufacture of flour and purchase and shipping of wheat enters largely into the prominent industries. The aggregate amount of wheat marketed here in 1883 was 800,000 bushels, which, it is thought, exceeds that of any other market in the State with the exception of Minneapolis. Eight flouring mills, with a capacity of 1,200 barrels of flour per day, and two capacious elevators, create a brisk competition, always securing to the producer the highest market price. The city draws a large trade in pork, principally from the wooded country extending for forty miles to the west, among whose groves and forests many of the finest farms in the county have been opened. It possesses a large number of fine water powers, which, supplied by the numerous lakes through which the Cannon River pursues its course, are seldom in want of a sufficient supply. Many of these, indeed, most of them, are already improved, but vacant powers in the city and vicinity may still be had. The Cannon River, rising in one of the numerous lakes twenty miles west of the city, and pursuing its course through the city eastwardly to the Mississippi, about forty miles to the east, is estimated to furnish a water power in every two miles of its course, and stretching along its banks the entire distance from Faribault to the Mississippi is a wheat field, which in the season of the great yield (1877) produced one-sixth of the entire wheat crop of the State, and was estimated by the Commissioner of Agriculture to produce the largest yield of any area of similar extent in the world.

The manufacture and export of furniture in the rough is a prominent branch of industry, two large furniture manufacturing establishments furnishing a ready market for the varieties of hardwood timber with which the neighboring forests abound, and large quantities of logs have, during the present winter, been purchased at the saw mills connected with these factories.

The woolen factory of C. H. Klemer manufactures superior cloths and blankets, which find a ready market in the surrounding country and in towns and villages in the vicinity, along the lines of the railroads which intersect at this point.

RESIDENCE OF A. L. HILL.

The Faribault Foundry and Windmill Company manufacture an excellent windmill, for which, having the exclusive patent, the demand exceeds the supply. Faribault wagons and carriages, noted for the excellence of their workmanship, are the product of several flourishing establishments, and are shipped to many of the towns and cities of the State.

Rice County, of which Faribault is the capital, was one of the earliest settled counties in the State. Its lands are under a high state of cultivation, nor have its farmers committed the common mistake of confining themselves to wheat. More than half of the county having been originally dense forest, the condition was unfavorable to the devotion of large tracts to wheat culture, which has been the bane of the prairie farmer, but afforded inducements for the raising of hogs and other domestic animals, and this section of the county was early distinguished for its diversified industry.

SEABURY DIVINITY SCHOOL.

Many fine stock farms exist in the country about Faribault, among which may be mentioned the picturesque situation of George M. Gilmore, Esq., to whose hospitality very many strangers who have visited the city in the past few years can testify. Surveying his herds of shorthorns, his trout ponds and fountains, and modern and commodious farm house and outhouses, the visitor is likely to forget that he is in a new country. The farm of George Robinson, Esq., also adjoining the city limits, merits special mention.

The dairy has not been neglected. The finest butter and cheese which

RESIDENCE OF T. H. LOYHED.

finds its way to the markets of St. Paul and Minneapolis will often, on inquiry, be found to be the product of Rice County herds. The State Dairymen's Association, which met in this city during the present year, brought out a display of dairy products seldom surpassed in quality.

Notwithstanding the fertility of the soil and the picturesque beauty of the county (for it is a county diversified with hill and dale, meadow and upland, forest, river and lake), farming lands in the vicinity of Faribault are surprisingly cheap, being from $15 to $40 per acre, while a few of the choicest stock farms, supplied with fine dwellings and capacious barns, reach, perhaps, $50 or $60.

Of course with such a tributary country trade could not be otherwise than brisk. The scene of bustle and activity usually presented by the streets of Faribault very greatly exceeds that generally observed in much larger Eastern towns. The block of substantial buildings, a view of which is given, indicates the prosperity which has justified them.

The plate glass fronts of the dry goods stores make a display which places our city in advance of most of its sister towns, and will compare favorably with any in the State, however large.

Its hardware and agricultural implement dealers, of whom there are

LIME STONE QUARRY.

many, have long enjoyed a very extensive and lucrative trade, and, as a consequence, stocks are to be found here of great extent and value. Neither is this nor the grocery trade confined entirely to retailing, for, while manufactures and retail trade are the principal business, yet jobbing in these branches is carried on by several houses of good financial character and capital.

Seated at the geographical center of a triangle, having its apex at the junction of the Mississippi and Minnesota Rivers at Mendota, in the vicinity of St. Paul, and its base on the Iowa line, with its angles at a prolongation of the Minnesota River from its great bend at Mankato and the Mississippi River, near La Crescent, Faribault has a climate equally

BRUNSWICK HOTEL.

adapted for corn and wheat, as the character of its agriculture, already mentioned, perhaps sufficiently discloses.

The fine limestone quarries already alluded to, of which its public buildings are constructed, supply, also, the Faribault marble, capable of receiving a high polish, as well as the material for large quantities of cement or water lime, although the latter has not yet been applied to use.

The Church of the Immaculate Conception (Catholic), the Cathedral of our Merciful Saviour (Episcopal) and Plymouth Church (Congregational) are good specimens of church architecture, the chancel of the Cathedral being said to be, with its stained glass windows and vaulted arches, the finest in the country. To the list should be added the elegant Memorial Chapel already referred to, with its imported furniture and fixtures, its font of Italian marble and its stained glass, the finest in the West. No expense has been spared to make it the architectural gem that it is. Notwithstanding the private educational institutions already mentioned, the public schools have not, as might be feared, been permitted to languish, but supply, from the primary to the high school, excellent educational privileges to more than a thousand pupils. A spacious central school building, supplemented by ward schoolhouses, furnishes fair, although, at present, somewhat inadequate accommodations for the rapidly increasing number of pupils.

Perhaps in nothing may Faribault more justly claim superiority than in her hotels. The Brunswick, the Arlington and the Allen Houses are all first-class establishments in fact as well as in name, while very many cheaper houses are well conducted and extensively patronized. The Brunswick is supplied with steam, gas, hot and cold water, and all modern conveniences; its spacious balconies afford a pleasing lounge for the tourist or pleasure-seeker, and it is elegantly furnished throughout with everything fresh and new, having been completed during the past year, and is regarded as a model of hotel architecture.

The city is lighted by gas, supplied, as is the water, by a private company. The fact that private companies can be induced to inaugurate and conduct such enterprises without municipal aid indicates the prosperity

which would alone justify such investments in a city of the size of Faribault.

The city has been peculiarly fortunate in the source of its water supply. Most of the larger towns and cities in which water-works have
been erected are dependent upon lakes or rivers, which, being exposed to
the sun, abound in unhealthy vegetable organisms, and are contaminated
by surface drainage, and the introduction of a host of substances tending

RESIDENCE OF REV. JAMES DOBBIN.

to impair their healthfulness. The Faribault Water-works Company
ventured upon the experiment of sinking a large well in the level plateau
forming the western outskirt of the city. It proved eminently successful,
as at the depth of twelve feet a stratum of coarse gravel was struck,
overlying white sand rock. A strong and constant current of pure cold
water was found rushing through this gravel bed, which constitutes a

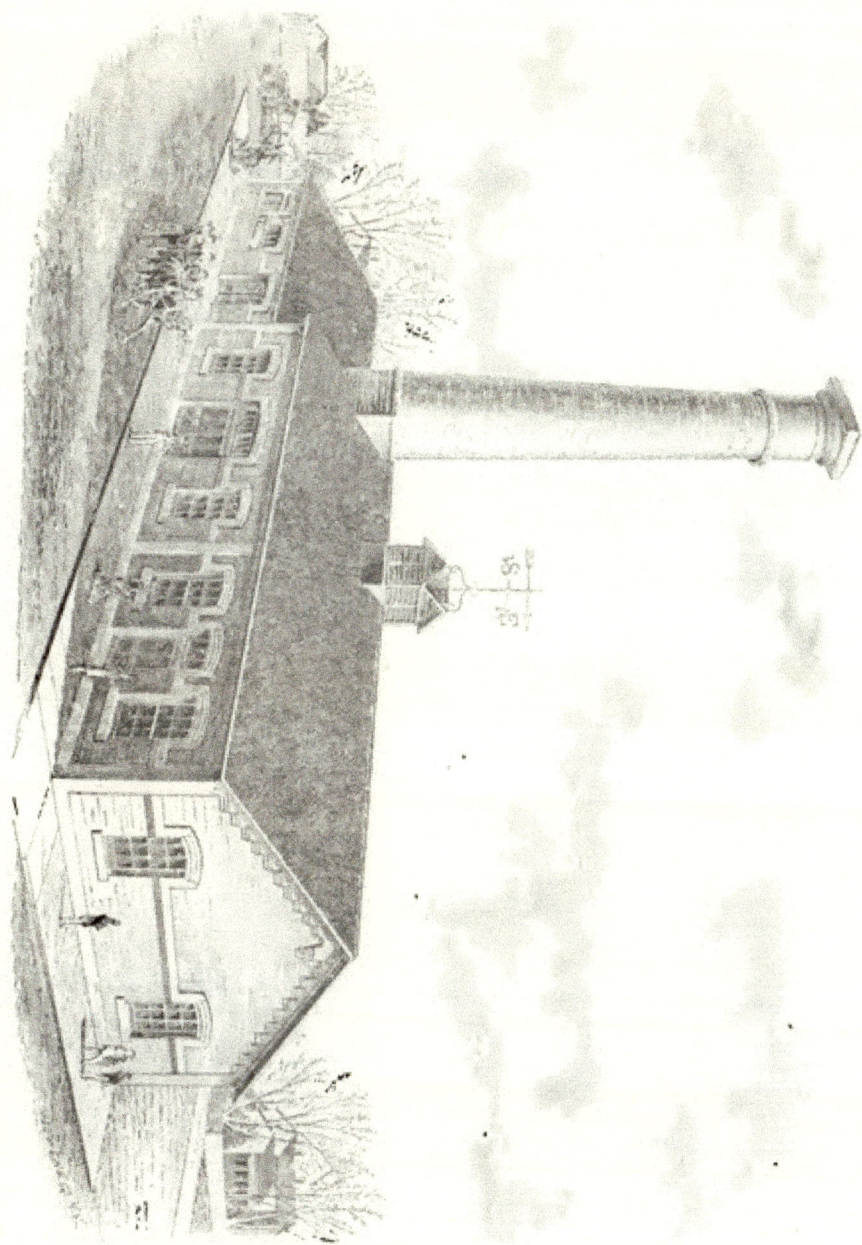

natural filter, with the force and volume of a subterranean river. The average depth of water in the well is twelve feet, and the tests made by the operation of the powerful steam pump show that the supply is practically sufficient for the utmost possible needs of the city, as the flow of the current into the well is estimated at 2,000,000 gallons a day. The water is forced through underground mains to a large reservoir situated on the heights east of the river and beyond the public institutions, at an elevation of 219 feet above the level of Main street in the city. The reservoir has a capacity of one and a quarter million of gallons. The water is supplied from it to all parts of the city, reaching the upper stories of the most elevated buildings, and affording most thorough protection in case of fire.

Two national banks, three breweries, two newspapers, representing the

RESIDENCE OF H. W. PRATT.

two principal political parties, and possessing excellent job offices, one operated by steam, and an opera house, may be mentioned in passing as among the existing institutions.

A view of one of the residence streets will be noticed, which will give an idea of the dense shade in which some of them are embowered. The close vicinity of the forest favored and stimulated the taste of the citizens in this direction, until the long avenues of trees which extend along the streets form one of its many attractions. In addition to these the public square, situated very nearly in the center of the city, is thickly planted with trees and supplied with an elegant fountain, the water for which is furnished gratuitously to the city by the water works company.

Of the many fine residences, lack of space has prevented the selection of but a few specimens, not the best or the poorest, but an average of the many which crown the hillsides into which the site of the city is broken.

The post office usually is a fair index of the prosperity of a town. During the last decade the gross receipts have doubled. There are two first class offices in the State, St. Paul and Minneapolis; and of the second class, Faribault stands well up in the list. The money order business amounts to $80,000 per year.

THE ABORIGINAL INHABITANTS.

Allusion has been made to the Wapekutis or Leaf Shooters, whose great council chamber, being a huge bark wigwam or tepee, called in the Indian dialect tepee tonka, or big tepee, was located on the shores of Cannon Lake, at or near the point shown in the view at Linden Park. The original name of this lake was Tetonka Tonah, or "Lake of the Village." As has been said, their forest habitations gave the name to this band of Dakotas. The history of the settlements of the white man, and the location of some of the most beautiful and thriving cities of the Northwest, show that the early emigrants, in search of locations of scenic beauty and natural advantages, found the best guides in the selection of the aboriginal tribes. The residence of Paypay, the second Chief of this band, was here, where he lived and died, enjoying, both among his own

SECOND STREET

people and their white brothers, a reputation for honesty, temperance and friendship for the whites. His descendants have always preserved the same character, with, perhaps, one exception. In the early years of the settlement his son, Chaska, was the fop of the band, and might often have been seen perambulating Main street, arrayed in all the splendors of war paint and feathers. Capt. John C. Whipple, an old resident, and the heroic artillerist whose volleys drove the howling fiends from the walls of the beleaguered fortress of Ridgeley in the gloomy days of the Sioux massacre, in 1862, who had often bestowed food upon this young warrior, was astonished at meeting him in the jungle, near the ferry at the lower, agency, still clad in his finery, but evidently meaning business, as his gun was pointed with murderous intent at the head of his quondam friend. He was afterward arrested, tried by the military tribunal organized for the purpose of trying the leaders of the insurrection, and condemned to death.

But in striking contrast with this ungrateful savage was the life of another descendant of the Chief, Taopi, who lived and died here. This Indian rescued 300 prisoners, women and children, from the hands of his bloodthirsty people, and delivered them in safety to Gen. Sibley. His fast friend and brother-in-law, who, crawling through miles of prairie grass and forest underbrush, dared a thousand dangers to bear the message to Gen. Sibley, which resulted in the happy deliverance of the captives, still lives among us, rejoicing in the name of Wachampamaza, a brave and good man, whose name should " fill the sounding trump of fame." Other members of his family still reside at the Indian village, located in a picturesque ravine just outside of the city limits. Although still adhering to the costumes and habits of their tribe, speaking no English and retaining the rude Dakota dialect, they are regular attendants at church, honest, industrious and self-supporting.

The traveler, on approaching the banks of the Cannon along the Hastings stage road, in 1855, as he reached the summit of the breezy heights which look down upon the present city from the east, would have witnessed a scene of marvelous beauty, enlivened by the presence of savage life. At his feet flowed the Twin Rivers, sweeping in a semicircle around the broad plateau on which the city now stands, reflecting in their bosom the dense foliage upon their banks, and forming a glowing crescent of sylvan scenery ; along the line of the present Main street, upon the sites of warehouses, stores and hotels, stretched a long line of Indian tepees or wigwams, while before them hung the kettle attended by the careful squaws, from which rose the savory steam from the Indian soup of dog ; their ponies, attached to the Sioux carriage, consisting of two

RESIDENCE OF F. A. THEOPOLD.

poles, the upper ends fastened by a rope to the pony, the others trailing on the ground, were feeding along the level prairie ; while up and down the banks of the stream dashed the naked warriors in the wheeling mazes of lacrosse, the Indian ball game ; and on the far western verge of the picture shimmered the placid waters of Tetonka Tonah and Wells Lakes.

Several years after, and when the rising town had reached upward of

CANNON LAKE, NEAR LINDEN PARK

2.500 inhabitants, when the tide of emigration was flowing into these verdant valleys, and "city lots were staked for sale, above old Indian graves," upon or near the site of the present Bethlehem Academy (a view of which is given), upon one of the most beautiful eminences in the present city, an Indian Grave Yard long remained, the bodies of the dead being raised upon scaffolding, in accordance with Indian custom, and surrounded with food, pottery and other offerings with which the relatives of the departed brave sought to smooth his way to the happy hunting grounds.

As late as this period, upon almost the exact site of the beautiful Memorial Chapel, a party of Dakota warriors returning from a successful raid upon their hereditary enemies, the Ojibways of the North, held their scalp dances and made the night hideous with their ringing war whoops ; for days the successful warriors paraded the streets with the bloody scalps of the slain, probably the reeking trophies of some cowardly ambuscade, bent upon hoops, and exultantly exhibited to the admiring eyes of the Wenonas of the tribe, as well as to the white citizens of the place. A dramatic incident, intended to illustrate the effects of Christianity upon these rude children of the forest, took place a few years ago in the Cathedral on the occasion of one of the general conventions which annually assemble here. A Dakota brave had become converted to Christianity, and entering the Divinity School as a student, died of consumption, that fell disease which is rapidly decimating the native red men. His funeral was appointed to take place during the session of the convention. At this convention there happened to be present from the northern parts of the diocese a half dozen young Ojibway clergymen, also converts to Christianity, under the devoted missionary efforts of Bishop Whipple ; these young Ojibways were the bearers of the remains of the dead Sioux to their last resting place. This, happening upon the spot where a quarter of a century before the ancestors of the deceased had paraded with demoniac glee the reeking scalps of the ancestors of the bearers, afforded a text for a thrilling discourse which we may be sure was not neglected. As the funeral cortege assembled in the chancel of the Episcopal Cathedral, which, with its groined arches and stained glass windows, is said to be the finest and most spacious chancel in the country, it presented, with these appropriate surroundings and in view of the contrasts referred to, a scene peculiarly impressive.

A sketch of the character of this would not be complete without some allusion to the lamented founder of our city, the late Alexander Faribault. The traveler whom I have imagined visiting these scenes in 1855 would have seen the Indian village diversified by a single frame building, the trading post of Mr. Faribault. This gentleman, allied by marriage with an Indian woman of this band of the Dakotas, early cast his fortunes among them, and was, so long as the tribe remained here, their wise and faithful benefactor, counselor and friend.

His was the type of a character which the wild, free life of the forest prairie is so well fitted to produce. Brave, generous, honorable, honest, free from guile himself and suspecting none of others, he was one of nature's noblemen, held in high esteem by the Indians, by all the brave men who with him had been the pioneers of the territory, as well as by the people who formed the new society which emigration brought with it. He lived until within the last year, and saw a flourishing city grow up upon the site of the old Indian village. His mansion, long the scene of his harmless life and generous hospitality, has become the north wing of the present institute for the education of the blind. The site of his trading-post is occupied by modern warehouses, whose brick, and iron and plate glass fronts furnish a contrast with his old trading-post as marked as that of the new civilization with the old barbarism. As he was the connecting link between the present and the past, his wise counsels were always sought to allay jealousies and quiet animosities between the two races. In the outbreak of 1862, when the town was guarded for many nights by relays of armed minute men under the command of Gen. Shields, of Mexican war renown, then a resident here, and whose blood-bought farm, as he was accustomed to call it, lies just outside of the city limits, Mr. Faribault's counsels were in great demand. Espousing the cause of the whites, although many of his Indian relatives were with the hostiles, he was in the expedition which fell into the ambuscade at Birch Cooley, and during those fearful hours when the little detachment, lying behind the bodies of their dead horses, gallantly maintained the desperate

CANNON LAKE—SARGEANT'S BAY.

struggle against myriads of hidden foes, while they listened with bated breath for the bugles of the relief party which finally rescued the survivors from a fate worse than death, he bore himself with that uncomplaining courage and fortitude which always characterized the man. The heroic defense which himself and his associates made at Birch Cooley, it is said, saved the city of Faribault from attack, as the band which were

RESIDENCE OF GORDON E. COLE.

on their way to devastate the scene of their early homes were drawn aside from their purpose by the detachment encamped at Birch Cooley, and its gallant defense detained them so long that their ultimate purpose was abandoned. Mr. Faribault's portrait hangs in the council room of the city, and his memory will be cherished by those who knew him and their descendants as long as the flourishing city which he founded and to which he gave its name shall continue.

NOTEWORTHY INCIDENTS OF THE CITY AND COUNTY.

The famous raid of the Younger brothers' band was made at North-field in this county, when they received the first check in a hitherto successful career, but two (supposed to be the James brothers) out of the band of eight escaping, and one of these severely wounded. The survivors were long imprisoned in the jail at Faribault, and at last tried and sent to the state prison for life. A view of the court house where the trial took place is shown. An armed volunteer company was organized by the Sheriff to protect the prisoners against lynching and prevent raids of their friends for their rescue. A city policeman was shot and killed by the patrol on guard, while attempting to approach the jail in the night.

The scene of Eggleston's "Mysteries of Metropolisville" is located in Faribault and vicinity. The beautiful lake upon which the sad accident occurred which constitutes the climax of the story, is about five miles distant, the drive to it being a very romantic one. The incident related by the author, of the capsizing of a sail-boat and the drowning of "little Katie," is no fiction, but one of the sad reminiscences of our history. M. Perritaut, of the novel, is the Mr. Faribault, to whose history brief reference has been made, and the other characters are mostly drawn from well-known personages in the early history of the place.

Rice County is the pioneer county in the manufacture of sugar from amber cane. The works of Seth H. Kenney, at Morristown, are still in successful operation, producing an excellent quality of pure syrup. The refinery at Faribault was the first completely equipped manufactory for the production of sugar from the sorghum plant established in the state, or it is believed the northwest. A superior article of granulated sugar was produced from it, but operations have been suspended, as it was not a financial success. The refinery, however, still remains, and it is believed that when the culture of amber cane shall have become more fully developed, work will be resumed with success. The first middlings purifier ever used in the country, and the pioneer machine of the great improvements that have revolutionized the milling industry of the North-

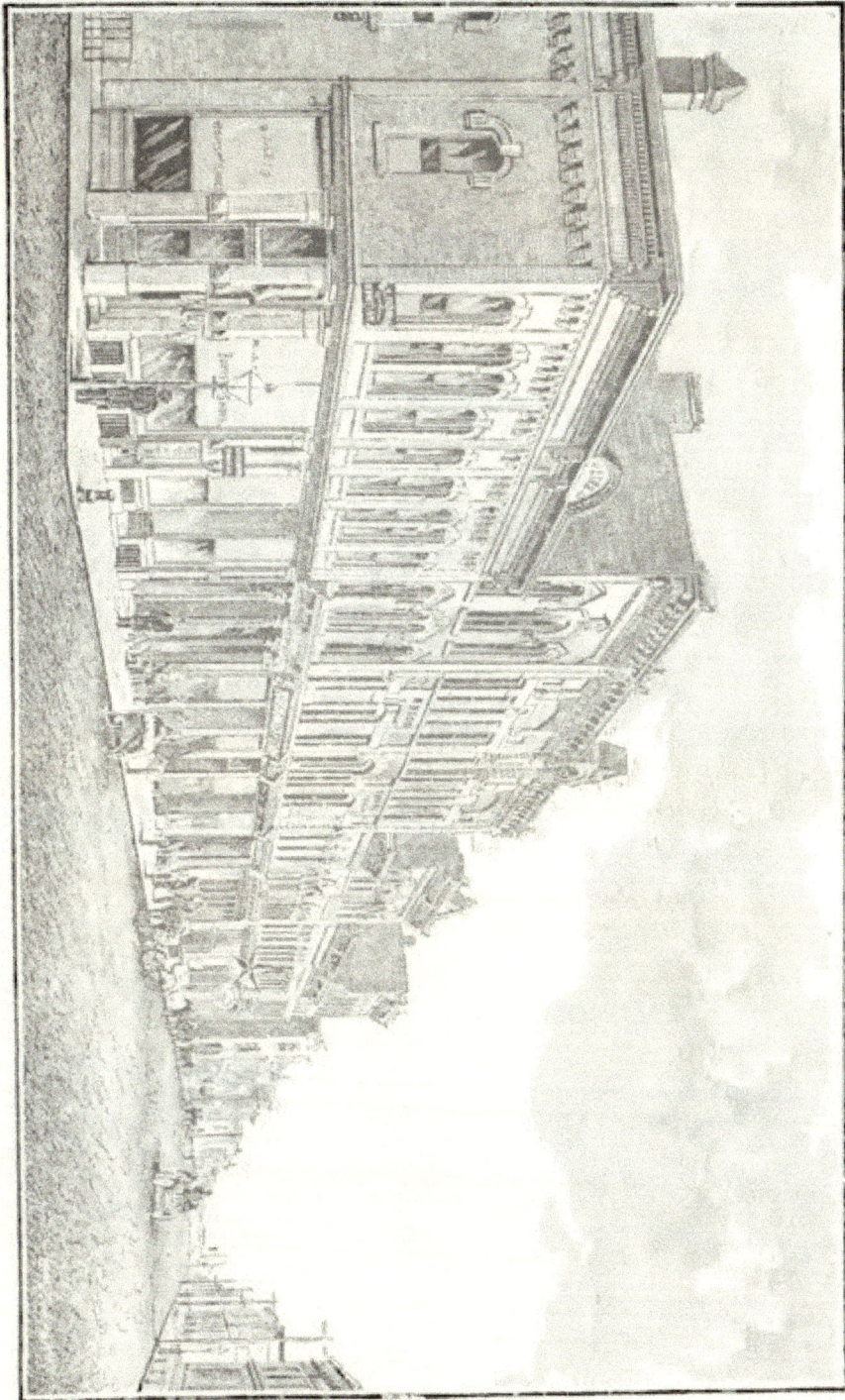

VIEW ON MAIN STREET

west and given to the product of Minnesota hard spring wheat its pre-
eminence, was built in Faribault, and first operated in one of our local
mills.

STATISTICS OF THE COUNTY.

To go a little into statistics : in the report of the tenth census it
appears that, in capital employed in manufacturing, Rice County stands
very nearly at the head of the counties of the State. Hennepin and
Ramsey, with the large cities of St. Paul and Minneapolis, are, of course,
largely in the lead, as is also Stillwater, the seat of the State's Prison and
the great manufactories of the Northwestern Car Co., and the Sey-
mour, Sabin & Co.'s works. After these come the great counties of
Goodhue and Winona, both nearly twice the geographical area of Rice,
and Rice stands next, having $975,000 invested in manufacturing as
against $1,105,000 for Goodhue, and $1,204,951 for Winona.

In horses and neat cattle she preserves about the same ratio to the
agricultural counties that she does to the manufacturing ones, only the
large counties of Winona, Olmstead, Mower, Goodhue, Fillmore and Blue
Earth being in advance of her, her aggregate amounting to 21,155.

A glance at the map of Minnesota, showing the twenty-six townships
of Goodhue, the twenty-five of Fillmore, twenty-two of Blue Earth and
eighteen of Olmstead, and the fourteen of Rice—and those more than
one-half originally dense forests—will indicate the significance of this
comparison, and place her at the head of the list, if her geographical area
is considered.

The same allowance for her smaller area will place her very nearly at
the head in wheat production. In this she stands tenth in the list of
counties, producing, in 1880, 905,514 bushels, as against 1,216,872 for
Winona, 1,461,674 for Wabasha, 1,135,704 for Stearns, etc., all the counties which exceed her being very much larger.

In the appraised value of her farm lands she aggregates $6,001,613,
and stands ninth on the list. Hennepin, with seven more government
townships, each a mile square, is estimated at only $8,017,191, and this
in the close vicinity to its capital city, the great wheat manufacturing
center at Minneapolis.

When it is remembered that, notwithstanding these comparisons, the prices at which Rice County lands can be bought are not higher but lower than others, if anything, it seems folly to seek those portions of the West where inflated values and speculative prices under the influence of a boom attract emigrants to settle upon wild lands, and town sites but recently platted which can only promise in return for fabulous prices for lots that a half a century hence they may have half the population that Faribault now has, and by the artificial cultivation of poplars, box elders, cottonwood and other quick-growing trees, create a faint imitation of the magnificent forest trees, groves and woods which dot the county of Rice, while her beautiful churches, her magnificent school edifices, her sparkling lakes and rivers they can never hope to rival.

The views in this little book are not fancy sketches. They are all made from photographs of the buildings or scenery to be represented. There is no need in any of them of embellishment. The effort has been made to present to the reader as perfect a representation as the skill of the artist can make of the actual scenes as they exist. And yet it is only just to say that there is a beauty and diversity of scenery in and about this picturesquely situated town that cannot be reproduced by the camera or the pencil. The object has been to keep as near to nature as possible, and to admit of no exaggeration.

BOATING PARTY AT CEDAR LAKE